MW01481932

When Your
Parents Divorce

A Handbook for Children
Whose Parents are Divorcing

by

Betty Clark

Copyright 1998

Betty Clark

ISBN 0-932796-89-3

Library of Congress Catalog No. 98-72127

Current printing of this edition (last digit):

9   8   7   5   4   3   2   1

Publisher—

Educational Media Corporation®
PO Box 21311
Minneapolis, MN 55421

(612) 781-0088

Production editor—

Don L. Sorenson

Graphic design—

Earl R. Sorenson

Artwork—

Cyndee Kaiser

Dedication

Dedicated to all the children who are trying to make sense of their parents' divorce and those parents who are willing to recognize their children's needs.

About the Author

Betty Clark, a retired teacher and public school counselor, a mother and grandmother, has seen first hand the pain and disillusionment faced by the children of divorce. Speaking candidly and with great depth of feeling, her comments in book form reflect her belief that children need help and understanding in dealing with major disappointments in their lives, particularly when parents are divorcing.

This is Betty's third book. She is a graduate from Indiana State University with a master's degree in education and counseling. Betty resides in Terre Haute, Indiana.

Educational Media Corporation®

Table of Contents

Educational Media Corporation®

Preface

It has finally happened to you. Quite without warning, your worst fears have come true. It has become a nightmare, but you are wide awake. Your world is shattered. The two people that you love most are calling it quits. The two people to whom you have always turned for comfort and answers are getting a divorce.

You feel positively terrible. You may even feel a little sick, stressful, and nervous. You don't want to talk about it; perhaps you can't. You have seen it happen to your friends, but you never thought such a dreadful thing could happen in your family. Even though you disagree with them at times, you still love your parents—both of them.

You may even be feeling a little guilty and asking yourself if, perhaps, you did something to make these two important people decide to live apart. Should you do anything to try to bring them back together? Is it too late? Can you stop this madness?

Your mind is racing with questions. Who's going to take care of you? Where will the other parent live? How is your life going to change? Will there be enough money for two homes? Will you be able to visit with your other parent? How often? Will you still have your grandparents? And, most of all, you wonder if your parents still love you. How will their falling out of love affect you—hurt you?

This book was prepared to help you answer these and many other questions young people face as they try to deal with their parents' divorce. Divorce is never easy, but usually when you realize exactly what is happening and what you should expect during and after the divorce, it need not be so tragic. You will be hurt, but you will survive this great change in your life.

This book also was designed to help you cope—to resolve or handle the confusion, hurt, and conflict you are facing now and will be facing as your parents live apart. It also will help you learn about "divorce" and how to survive your parents' breakup.

When you have read through this book, the next thing you should do is to insist that *both* of your parents read the entire book. They may not want to—perhaps they are too emotional at this point—but reading it could help them to understand your feelings and needs.

As you look at your actual situation and plan for the changes which will likely take place as a result of your parents' divorce, you will discover coping skills you never thought possible. You'll even learn how to deal with the new people that may come into your life. You will find yourself "growing up." This book will help you. And, just as important, this book will help your parents.

Educational Media Corporation®

Chapter 1
The Bitter Truth

Finding out that your mother and father were separating was probably the shock of your young life. No, it's worse than that. They are not just separating, they are planning a divorce. You might as well learn to say it. The words stick in your throat, tears start to burn, and you can hardly believe it, but your parents are going to get a divorce.

You are worried and uneasy because you don't know what to expect. You know of other families where the parents have separated, and it wasn't all that nice. People gossiped and the children in the family were usually angry. It wasn't fun for anyone.

It's difficult for you to know exactly what is going to happen between these two people that you have been living with for years. Exactly how different will it be? How will the family change? What can you expect? Just how does divorce really work?

To be certain, there will be changes and no two families are alike. No two situations are the same. Just as no

> *No divorce is exactly like another.*

two sets of parents are the same, and no two children are the same, so it is with divorce. No divorce is exactly like another. There are always different circumstances.

And, just as there are all kinds of divorce situations, there also are different kinds of problems that bring on the separation. Often there are deep feelings of anger in one or both of the parents. There may be painful emotional scars that divorce won't fix. Divorce may be the only sensible answer. Still it is scary.

There are different ways that parents tell their children about their divorce. Perhaps you learned about the separation when you came home from school. It was clear to you at the very moment you walked through the door that something was wrong. You could tell from their strange, sad, expressions that something was wrong. Maybe you never even suspected trouble and now, all at once, they are telling you that one of them is leaving. Even in this happiest of homes, something has gone wrong.

 Educational Media Corporation®

These two loving and wonderful people are telling you, as kindly as possible, that their marriage is over.

Or maybe you had overheard their quarrels or some of their conversations about splitting up. You knew something was going to happen before they told you the whole story.

No doubt they told you not to worry. They said everything would be all right. They were telling you the truth. Everything will be all right. What they did not tell you was how difficult it was going to be.

Perhaps the divorce was something you'd been dreading for weeks, even months. You remember the quarrels, the unhappiness, the violence, and the threats that one parent would make to the other. You recall the hateful name calling, the shouting, and the tears. When they finally came to the decision to get a divorce, it really didn't come as much of a surprise. You were expecting it. That's all either parent had talked about for a long time. They both had been so distressed, so angry, and so disappointed that you felt their marriage was doomed to failure.

Still, the hurt was there all the same. It didn't matter whether your father took you aside and explained that he is moving out, or whether your mom and dad faced you together with kindness in their hearts. Either way it hurt. You love them both and now they are going their separate ways.

It doesn't really matter at this point who is actually to blame for the split. It's happening and it's no fun. Also, it isn't important what caused the divorce. It may be because of alcoholism, unemployment, drugs, or the fact that one of your parents is having an affair. Whatever has brought your parents to this point, it is difficult for the children in the family—it is difficult for you.

Perhaps your parents simply don't love each other anymore. They may want to start new lives. One or both of your parents may be having a mid-life crisis. They may be 35 or 40 years old and that scares them.

Whatever the cause, it still hurts and, while they are putting their plans in order, you have to deal with your own problems. Sometimes it seems that your parents don't even notice you. Do they know you are there? Do they realize that your life is going to be different?

They may be too caught up in their divorce to realize that you are hurting. You may have to give them some time. Perhaps they will come to know that you need some heart-to-heart talks with them. They need to comfort you.

During these early stages of the divorce you will find your-self going through a number of emotional changes. For instance, when your parents did get around to telling you all about their plans, you were, no doubt, confused and angry. Sometimes you just don't want to hear about it. You prefer to shut it out and maybe it will go away.

You may have lost your appetite and aren't really interested in the things you used to like. You may have trouble falling asleep. It isn't even fun to be around your friends anymore.

When you came to realize that the divorce was not going to go away, and after you had time to think about it, you probably noticed a small change in yourself. You may still have a lot of anger and many worries, but you probably sense a small change in your feelings and your attitude. You are beginning to cope. You are moving away from the confusion.

Believe it or not, your emotions will change day by day. What is important to remember is that your feelings of hurt and disappointment are normal. You are normal. You have a right to be sad. You are not being disloyal to your parents by having some angry thoughts.

You are facing what almost half of the children in the United States are facing—or have faced—the breakup of a family. Fortunately, it's not the end of the world; it's not going to keep you from becoming a fine, respected adult—a kind, reasonable person. It's not going to keep you from ever being happy again. It's not going to ruin your life unless you let it.

> *You are facing what almost half of the children in the United States are facing.*

It does mean, though, that a difficult obstacle—a speed bump—has been placed on your road to growing up. You are going to have to climb over some rocky paths. It will help you if you can learn to look at your parents' divorce as a fairly large hill that you must climb to get on with your own life. However, try not to make it a mountain too big to climb.

Certainly, you must not let your parents' action affect the real you, a young person with plans and dreams. It mostly means that you have to study your situation, pick up the pieces, and face your future bravely. Maybe it won't be so bad.

Fortunately, there are some steps that you can take to help you stay on track, to help you make good choices, and to help you grow up wiser, better prepared, and ready for the next crisis. Let's think about it. Let's start making plans that will work for you while your parents work out their divorce.

Chapter 2
Family History

The first few days, hours, and minutes after hearing the news of your parents' divorce are strange. The house seems different. The television still has the same old favorite programs, but something is wrong. Everything looks the same, but there is a change in the house.

You may fold your clothes a little neater, a little slower, and more carefully as if that will help. You may stare at your room a little more, thinking about it, remembering.

Your mind may wander while you are trying to read your assignments or do your homework. As you leave the house for a little while, you may give it a slow, thoughtful glance. How long will you be living at this address? It has been your home for quite a while. Will that change?

You may notice that you are watching the other members of the family a little closer. You may want to hug the younger children a little more. You may want to ignore your parents. You may want to show them a little more or a little less love.

You may be angry. You may be sad. You are lonely. You are wondering what to do next. You feel terrible. You may be blaming yourself. Hopefully, you are not. Children are not to blame for the actions of the adults. Yet, still you wonder if you have done some really harmful things or said some mean remarks. Are you to blame in any way?

So what is the next step? At this point you may have already realized that moping about, crying, throwing a tantrum (fit), slamming doors, or ignoring your parents really doesn't seem to be very helpful. What else can you do to get over this terrible mood that has taken over your body?

Certainly, the first step is important. It involves figuring out exactly where to look for help. It may be a difficult step for you because it means that you must begin facing the problem. That's the only way you can truly make some decisions on how you are going to handle this most unhappy situation. You have to face the problem, confront the fact that your loved ones are going their separate ways.

To whom should you turn when your world is turned upside down? Whom can you trust? What action should you take besides just sitting in front of the television thinking about it, thinking about what is happening to the family?

One help may be right under your feet. If you have a family pet, a dog or a kitty, you have an edge. There is quite a bit of comfort just being with your animal friend. As the two of you sit together, not speaking the same language, you can still feel the closeness and the value of that togetherness. You love that animal almost like a person. That animal shows love for you, too.

You are lucky to have each other when things are bad. Your pet doesn't ask any questions and certainly doesn't give any answers, nor does the pet put you down, make you uncomfortable about your feelings. Your pet seems to understand. You have each other with which to share quiet moments together.

But then what? Or what if there isn't a family pet? Maybe pets aren't allowed where you live. What can you do? Where can you go to sort out your feelings and get back on your feet, get over your disappointment, and get back to being your old self? How do you face this divorce?

As soon as you can bring yourself to do it, you really must face the problems of dealing with both of your parents and their feelings. You love them both and you are stunned and disappointed by their action, but how do you handle it?

It is possible that one parent is easier to talk to than the other. Perhaps one is closer to you than the other. Maybe both of them are ready to listen to your fears. Maybe neither of them will discuss anything with you.

Perhaps there have already been some family discussions and nothing good came from them. Maybe you had a chance to express your feelings; maybe you did not. Maybe the family discussions always turned into shouting matches and small wars, bringing out the dreadful arguments and hurt once more. Their quarrels and violence often scared you.

It is easy to see that the better the communication is between family members, the easier your new life style will be to handle. But, if you are not able to have reasonable discussions, you will just have to tough it out. Time will change that, too.

Being in the dark about the future makes everything that much harder. You will get along much better if your parents will share their thoughts with you and help you know what's happening now, what's going to happen in the future, and when the big changes will begin.

Fortunately, most parents realize that their children need to talk to someone. When you are feeling really lost and depressed, it truly helps to vent your feelings, to talk it over. The problem is that many times parents aren't sure of their own plans, their own feelings. All they really know is that they are splitting up. They can't give you answers if they don't have them. They need time, too.

Next to sharing with your parents, why not talk to your grandparents? Remember them? They are the folks who spoiled you as a little child, overlooked your mistakes, and often gave you advice whether you wanted it or not. These kind folks would love to hear from you. They will listen, talk to you on the phone, and read your letters. They will most likely understand your sadness and shock. They will welcome a chance to express their concern for your situation. They will welcome a chance to tell you of their continued love for you.

It is possible that one or more of your grandparents have been divorced. It's not uncommon today. You may already have step-grandparents. You can see that it hasn't ruined their lives. They seem like pretty content, reasonably happy adults. If not, maybe they were just born disagreeable and their divorces had nothing to do with it. Maybe they just made some poor choices in their own lives. They will want you to learn from their mistakes.

Now is a good time for you to see the importance of making the wisest choices possible in your own life. Don't let yourself get into a mess because of someone else's problems. Don't let your parents' divorce force you into making stupid decisions now. Don't let your anger and disappointment cloud your thinking. Try to keep your mind clear and your actions sensible. Keep your head on straight.

> *Don't let your parents' divorce force you into making stupid decisions.*

Try to remember that your parents have brought you this far and parents and grandparents usually stand ready to comfort their children and grandchildren when given an opportunity. Your parents are getting a divorce from each other. Your parents are not divorcing *you*. They are still going to be your mother and father. Your grandparents are still going to be your grandparents.

If, by chance, you do not have grandparents, or if they are not a part of your life presently, this approach to your fears will not work. You will, however, find other solutions.

Some things will change, but just because your parents are going to be living in different houses doesn't mean that you will stop being a family. Yours will be a different family, but you will be a family all the same. Your parents will continue to be concerned about your present welfare and your future, just as you are concerned about them.

They will want to spend time with you. They will want to be your parents and grandparents wherever they are. Your parents have simply come to a parting of their ways, but they are going to be a very big part of your life for many years.

You must keep in mind that this is a difficult time for your parents as well. They may be so caught up in their own worries and frustrations that they don't always seem to be concerned about you, but they are. In their hearts they are more concerned than ever. They may not show it, but they are.

This is a difficult time for your parents as well.

While they are in this stressful situation, they need to know that you will still care about them after the divorce is final. They are probably just as upset as you and need your kindness and patience. And, in many cases, your parents may be trying to deal with a fair amount of guilt and uncertainty.

Reassure them if you can that you understand their needs and that you realize that all of you are still going to be a family. You will be, in fact, "parenting" your parents. You shouldn't have to do it. They should be comforting you, but it can be your gift to your distressed family.

Let them know that you understand that love isn't turned on or off like a faucet. It can be left on all the time, even through a divorce. Hopefully, they will feel the same way too.

It will be a changed family, but life is full of change. It doesn't have to be stressful for a long, long time. Things will work out. You'll soon be on a track to the future of which you can be proud. You also can be proud of yourself for helping other family members. You are growing up fast.

Chapter 3
Other Kinfolk

Besides your parents, another place that you can turn is to your other family members. It is the most natural thing in the world for you to talk to your brothers and sisters. That would include any half-brothers and half-sisters as well. These people are all involved in what happens to the family.

These are the people with whom you have shared your joys and sorrows in the past. They know what is happening within the family already. They are going to be affected or changed by the divorce just as you will be. You will, no doubt, talk to them about the divorce.

Often, in your room at night—especially if you share a room, you will be wondering about the divorce and talking about the split-up. Younger brothers and sisters will look to their more grown-up siblings for advice and comfort.

If you happen to be the eldest child or one of the older children, this responsibility will fall on you. The little ones will automatically turn to you if given a chance to do so. You will be a hero or heroine to them for a time as they look to you for comfort.

It's not an easy responsibility. Not only will you have to deal with your own fears and concerns, but you will have to try to comfort your younger brothers and sisters. If you think you are scared and worried, consider their fears. The breakup of the family will disturb the younger children beyond belief. They will need your reassurance very much.

> *You will have to try to comfort your younger brothers and sisters.*

They will come right out with their questions such as, "Where will we live?" and "Will we be separated?" They will ask the questions that you were afraid to ask. They may ask you, over and over, "Who will you live with, Mommy or Daddy?"

Strangely enough, you will find that by helping them, talking to them, and explaining the problem to them, you will be helped as well. As you teach them and guide them through this murky business, you will find an inner strength as you build hope in your younger siblings.

They need to hear you say, "It will be okay." You will build a sense of togetherness as you come to their rescue. They will see you as their leader, their role model.

If you are not the eldest sibling, then you will be able to turn to the oldest member to talk it out. It is very important that you truly try to be kind and helpful to this older sibling. Even if you have had quarrels in the past and you find this older sibling a little pushy and bossy at times, try to remember that this brother or sister may be even more stressed than you. The older sibling may have more responsibility. He or she may be doing more of the housework, more cooking, more baby sitting—even more worrying.

Whether you are one of the older children or not, as a member of a divorcing situation, everyone in the family should try to keep peace. Each person should try to make things go as well as possible. Maybe you can help the problem by just being good natured and pleasant. Try not to spread more gloom. Whether or not you actually end up helping anyone in the family, at least no one can say that you were unkind when they needed your patience.

It is possible that your older siblings may not live at home any more. Older siblings who have moved out are usually good contacts—good people to whom you can talk about this family crisis. They are not children anymore and, as adults, they can probably shed lots of light on the problem. They know the family well and will add to your understanding of what is happening to the family.

Try to contact your older siblings. Perhaps your parents will let you visit, stay overnight, or spend some time with an older, perhaps wiser, sibling. Every situation is different, but if it is possible, go and talk to an older member of the family.

Such actions will help you in more ways than you can imagine. For one thing, you will be taking a little time off from the hurtful scenes that you find at home. It will give you a fresh outlook on dealing with your feelings.

You can draw some strength from family members who no longer live at home. If you are lucky, this person will entertain you, take you out to eat, go to a movie, rent a video, and help you forget your problems. It will be a pleasant change. You will find that this brother or sister is very concerned for you and your feelings.

Don't forget other family members. Besides the very close members of the family, you may have a favorite aunt and uncle or some cousins that would enjoy a visit from you. These are people you have known all your life. You will find talking to them will help you if it does nothing but let you air out your problems.

Aunts and uncles may not want to discuss family problems in great detail, but they will probably be very understanding and kind. Go to them for a short visit if you can. Remember, your parents are divorcing each other. You will still be related to these other people. They are still a part of your extended family. They will remain a part of the family for years and years. Feel free to meet with them and talk with them as you have done in the past. It's all in the family.

In later years when you have children of your own, you will want these people in your life. You won't lose them unless you want to. You may find that they are very sensitive to your needs. They may be kinder and closer than you think. Give them a chance.

Things will change, even your bad moods. Just work on it. Do what you can to help the other family members. It will be to your advantage or benefit to become the best kind of person that you possibly can, even in this unhappy situation.

However, you are not Superman or Superwoman and you are not expected to perform miracles. Tomorrow is another day and you will be ready for it. The shock will be over soon and you'll be back on track. It will be a somewhat different track, but you can make it the best track.

 Educational Media Corporation®

Chapter 4
Friends

Another natural place for you to turn in a time of divorcing parents is to your friends. Children, when there is a serious problem, want to seek comfort from their friends. That's one of the many advantages of having a truly good friend. You have each other.

You may have only one young person your age who seems to understand the real you. You seldom have over two or three truly close and trusted friends.

In any case, this circle of friends can be a big help to you as you sort out your feelings. If you do feel that you can trust your close friend or friends, and sincerely believe that they will be tight-lipped about what you are sharing, you are most fortunate. A good friend, one that you can trust, will help you unload your fears and talk it out.

This friend will let you *dump* on him or her. A true friend will understand. True friends will not repeat your inner-most secrets unless you give them permission, unless you tell them that they may.

You need answers that will not offend them, but answers that will stop their questions.

It may be that some classmates are curious or simply nosy. Be a little careful. They may just be prying. They may need or want some excitement in their own lives. Your parents are getting a divorce. That is news and they want to talk about it.

So beware, you must watch what you say to some of these *so-called* friends. You probably don't want to go into detail with anyone except your closest friends.

To handle those nosy folks, you do need to build some classic answers to their questions. You need answers that will not offend them, but answers that will stop their questions. You can do it. You can plan what to say.

Don't be too blunt and crude or you will make them even more curious. Instead, give them a guarded reply—a good, short answer without telling them anything of real importance. Think up some good replies. You have the right to discourage nosy friends and classmates.

Some such answers might be: "My parents are having some problems, but that's nothing new," or "My parents are having problems, but they don't tell me anything." When they say that they have heard that your parents are splitting up, you can simply say, "Maybe, but nothing has really been decided." Or, "There are some problems," is quite a good answer.

You really need to begin your list immediately. Have a ready answer of your own choosing. Have a good friend help you.

Most of all, don't tell halfway friends anything personal if you don't trust them. If you have any reason to distrust them or if they have betrayed you in the past, keep private information away from them. It is difficult to tell how they will repeat it.

Of course you can't tell them that you don't trust them. They would pry even more. Just work on your ready answers. If you become pressured, you can always put a stop to it by saying, "See you later," at which point you just walk away. Have some place you need to go. "I've gotta get somewhere right away. See you later."

Besides your friends, hopefully you have a teacher, coach, or school employee who is close enough to you that you can talk. If you are having a really bad time of it, you might want to mention it to one or more of these caring adults.

They may be able to help you with your studies, talk with you, or perhaps refer you to someone else. Most school people truly care for their students and are willing to help them through difficult times. They may suggest that you see a counselor.

Whether you are referred to a counselor or whether you go to see a counselor on your own, it's a very positive step. A counselor can set aside certain times for you to talk things out. You can express your concerns and feelings. Often the counselor can ease your pain by pointing out options, things that you can do.

A counselor will keep things confidential, private. You can talk freely, say what you want, and your counselor will not share the information. There is one possible exception. If your counselor feels your life is in danger, or that you are about to run away or break the law, he or she will have to do something for your safety. Usually the counselor can help you find answers so that you won't want to break the law or act foolishly.

A coach is another good resource if you happen to be involved in sports. Your coach will probably spot that something is wrong and can help you understand that life goes on, changed, but not so changed as you might imagine. You are still going to be in that sport, whether your parents are divorced or not.

Furthermore, your coach will be there to assist you before and after practice and help arrange for rides to and from the practice if he or she knows the circumstances. Coaches have a lot of freedom when it comes to actually helping their team members. They are usually good listeners because they care about children.

If things are really difficult for everyone—parents and children—a family counselor or therapist can be called. This is a professional service and your parents would have to agree that they need help. This is sometimes difficult for parents to do. They generally have made up their minds and do not want any outside interference.

You are indeed fortunate if your parents agree to seek help to solve their marriage problems. Counselors can help the children deal with the divorce, even if parents are not willing to talk with the counselor.

Often parents are afraid to take the problem to a professional counselor. It may cost them money they don't want to spend. They may be afraid this professional will try to keep them together and they don't want to stay together. One parent may agree to go, while the other refuses. All families are different.

They may have other fears that they can't talk about. Their actions may be too painful, even for them. But, every divorcing parent should seriously consider using a trained therapist or family counselor. Divorce is a big step, changing many lives for better or worse. The counselor can help all the members. It is your parents' decision as to whether or not to seek professional help.

It's amazing how many people stand ready to help you through all kinds of problems.

If money is the main reason for their not wanting to see a counselor, it is possible that your family can get help at very little cost. Certain agencies charge for their services according to the income of the family. It could end up costing very little to have this help. Again, this is up to your parents. It is, however, something that you can mention when talking to either of them.

There's another place that you can turn. If you belong to a church or youth group, you can find friends and leaders who can show you that they care. There are a number of people in these organizations who realize how blue and unhappy divorce can make children feel. One such person may have handed you this book.

In any case, do not hesitate to talk to your pastor, priest or rabbi. They are trained counselors who will gladly listen to your problems and help you to cope with your situation.

It's amazing how many people stand ready to help you through all kinds of problems. Of course, you have to seek them out. They won't just go by your house and knock on your door. If such a person does show up at your door, you may be sure that someone wanted to help and referred that person to your family.

If you take some positive steps on your own, you will find you are dealing very well with the trauma of divorcing parents.

There is one important thing to realize at this time, perhaps the most important of all. This is not the time to let your school work or your school activities slide. It won't help you to let yourself get lazy about studying. It will be your successes in school and the wise decisions that you make now that will help you in this crisis and others that will come into your life.

Stay on top of your school work, sports, and other activities. You won't be sorry. There is no sense in letting your grades go down the tube just because your life is changing. You are still a team member, whether your parents are divorcing or not.

You want to know that you did the best you could. You continued to turn in assignments, often through tears, but you did them. You want to know that you seriously built your own future, even when others made it difficult.

Knowledge will see you through. Try to learn for the sake of learning; try to build your skills. Don't just throw in the towel because you are having a bad time. Make good things happen while you deal with the bad.

Take your time, study your situation, and soon you will be in control again. Soon, much sooner than you ever thought possible, you will smile again. You will get on with your own life and not let your parents' divorce make you angry or sad. You may feel sorry for their unhappiness, but their actions don't have to make you less than you can be.

Educational Media Corporation®

Chapter 5
The Closed Family

When you are thinking about *talking things over,* there are some other important things to think about. One thing to think about is you, your personality, and what is right for you as a person.

It may be that you are the kind of a person who doesn't open up easily. You like to keep things to yourself. Maybe you are a bit of a loner and you can't see yourself solving your problems by talking them out with anyone. It may be a family thing—not talking to others outside the family. No matter. That's okay, too.

It is true that some children can and will handle the stress and disappointment of their parents' divorce all by themselves. Often, these children have already faced many disappointments. They believe keeping hurts to themselves, building a shell or wall, keeps away more hurt.

> *Some children can and will handle the stress and disappointment of their parents' divorce all by themselves.*

Maybe it's just that you are naturally shy. Who can say why a child is a loner and can't share much with friends? These children have learned to just keep everything to themselves and they like it that way.

Or you may be one of those children who is so hurt and angry about the whole thing that you just want to be left alone, to be left alone at least for a while. That's no problem as long as you are careful not to bury your feelings so deep that you become physically sick. When you are very alone with no one with whom to talk, you can become so stressed that it can make you sick.

If you are simply a natural *loner,* protect yourself by keeping involved in your hobbies or reading, whatever, so as to avoid letting the divorce make you physically ill. If you don't have a hobby of any kind, maybe you should find one—start looking: drawing, sewing, crafts, comics, sports cards, whatever.

Building a shell around yourself is not so unusual. You are not expected to be full of fun and games right now. Even the most outgoing and happiest of children is not likely to be the life of the party—the school clown or cutup—at this particular moment. The family is splitting up and each child has to deal with it in his or her own fashion. It's not very funny.

Nor is it uncommon for children not to want to talk about what is happening. It's perfectly normal. They may even think that if they don't talk about it, it will go away. That's a common reaction, too.

Sometimes, parents *do* change their minds and decide to make the best of their marriage. However, more often than not, the divorce does not go away. The court action has been filed, the lawyers are working on it, the papers have been served, but you don't have to talk about it until you are ready.

You can comfortably take a *wait and see* attitude. In any case, one thing is certain. Whether you talk about it with anyone or deal with it on your own, you must not blame yourself. It's not your fault and the actions of your parents can't make you any less of a person than you want to be. Just remember, your parents are divorcing each other. They are not divorcing you.

There is another important thing you may have to consider as you try to deal with the situation. Let us suppose that your family is a quiet, *closed* family that does not want *any* outside discussion about the divorce. What if you have been told *not* to talk about it to anyone under *any* circumstances? Where can you turn for some kind of information and help? What's a lonely, disappointed, and confused child to do if your parents have forbidden you to share your feelings with an outsider?

If you find you are in a *closed* family, you will have to work through your parents' divorce quite differently. Maybe you can understand this family value or trait. It's been a family thing for a long time.

For instance, all too often if there is an alcoholic or drug addict in the home, these problems are not things any family wants to discuss. Families tend to protect the addict or alcoholic. Losing a job or a parent having an affair also are problems families try to keep secret for as long as they can. It is guarded information.

So it is with the *closed* family that must deal with a divorce. You are told, "Don't talk about it." Or a parent may say, "We don't wash our dirty clothes in public." A parent may even insist on you not telling anyone at school; that includes your friends. What happens then?

Let's hope your *closed* family is a warm and *close* family and you don't need to seek outside friends or help. Hopefully your parents are comforting you and will share their thoughts with you and your brothers and sisters. Perhaps your usually secretive parents are keeping you aware of the changes that are about to happen. Perhaps they have already taken time to talk to you, to ease your pain. Perhaps not.

If your family is close and understanding, your parents will comfort each other and help you and your siblings as they work out their plans. You will know what's going on. You will know what to expect. You will work things out through your private, *closed,* though, close, kind, and sharing family.

Even in a closed family it is most likely that the rules will be relaxed very soon. When one of the parents actually leaves the house and sets up a second household, the rules will change.

The remaining parent in the home will *have* to have a more *open* attitude.

With the divorce the rules will change because your parents and your parents' lives are changing. Even the parents in a *closed* family will have to face the fact that a divorce is almost impossible to keep private. One or both of them will have to change their ways of thinking.

Certainly it will not be a secret anymore when one parent has a different address and telephone number. Second numbers may be given to the school in case of an emergency. There really is

> *Neighbors will be the first to know when there is a pending divorce.*

no reason to be upset if the school officials need new addresses. You want to be available at any of the numbers. Your friends can call you at either parent's house.

Neighbors will be the first to know when there is a pending divorce. They soon get the picture when there is only one car in the driveway where there used to be two. Very soon, even in a closed family, you will not have to hide your feelings. You don't have to tell the folks next door if your parents have asked you not to tell. The neighbors will find out on their own.

In the meantime, if you are in a closed family and were told not to discuss your fears with anyone outside the home, there are places you can go to better understand your situation. The school library and the public library have an unbelievable amount of books and videos that cover divorce and its effect on children. You know you will be affected. Let books and videos spell it out for you.

Churches often have material in the vestibule, lobby, or reading room. Take advantage of their brochures and booklets. There is good data on those pamphlets—addresses, suggestions, and so forth.

You can tell a librarian what kind of material you are looking for without actually disobeying your parents' rules. Librarians may wonder why you want these materials, but they will more than likely think you are doing a report for an assignment.

If you don't have a VCR at home, the library will provide one for you. Take advantage of these books and videos until such time that you can tell your friends or some other person who can help you. You are not alone. It will only be a matter of time. You can do it.

Remember, even if you are discouraged and sad, both of your parents need to know that you will still care about them after the divorce is final. They are probably just as upset during this trying period as you are and they need your kindness and understanding more than ever. And, you need their love at this critical time.

Reassure them, if you can, that even though you are just a child, you understand their needs. You realize that all of you are still going to be a family. That's you doing the parenting again, but it will help. Maybe your parents will see that you are trying to cooperate and be even more helpful than before.

Yours will still be a changed family, but life is full of change. It doesn't have to be stressful for a long time. You can still look forward to a great future.

Educational Media Corporation®

Chapter 6
The Missing Parent

In a matter of a few days or weeks after your parents decided to get a divorce, the real changes begin. At some point in the divorce proceedings, one parent leaves the home and settles somewhere else.

Being in the house without that person is one of the toughest things you have to take. As a rule, those first few days without both parents are trying and troublesome.

The house seems strange. You may have lived in the same place for many years, but now it is different. It is your first night in this house when one of the members has gone—moved out. It is usually the father who leaves, but it could be either parent. Remember, every situation is different.

You lie in your bed that first night thinking of the good times in the past. They didn't always seem like good times, but looking back, you

> *That first morning after the actual separation most likely will be strange and dismal.*

feel they were better than now, with one parent living somewhere else. Unless that parent was an absolute monster, you will miss this person. You bonded with this person.

Even if a child has been abused—mentally, physically, or sexually by a parent—that child often will try to help that parent, defend the parent. The child still finds the bond very strong and binding. Even a child who has been deeply damaged cannot bear to see the missing parent hurt or in trouble. If you find yourself in this same situation, your pity and concern is normal. You have a natural attachment to this person. Of course, you care.

With one parent out of the home, you realize that even a simple thing like eating breakfast will be different. In the past there were times when you didn't even take time to eat breakfast. Now it seems impossible to enjoy a meal.

Or perhaps it will go the other way. You may find that eating becomes your main source of enjoyment, especially if you can't talk about your problems. You may find yourself eating when you aren't hungry. You could even find comfort in having a *full* tummy. It may seem to be a good way to be loved. You may feel it helps take the place of the missing person.

Should that happen, you can quickly see that eating constantly can't help you. It can't be a benefit to you. It can only cause you more grief. Hopefully you will be able see that overeating can only cause you pain. It will not bring your parents back together again. Overeating will not take the place of loneliness, except for those moments when you are actually eating. Then you must eat all the time to satisfy the hunger you feel from the loneliness. It's a bad solution. Don't fall for it.

That first morning after the actual separation most likely will be strange and dismal. During that first evening at the dinner table or at the fast food restaurant, everything will seem different with only part of the family there to enjoy it.

The first few days without your noncustodial parent may still seem long and lonely. The noncustodial parent—the missing parent—is the one with whom you are not living. That's the parent who has moved from the house. That's the parent you will immediately miss.

Even if that missing parent has been a troublesome, unkind parent, you will worry. You will wonder about where that parent is, what that parent is doing, and whether or not that parent is thinking of you. You will sense a feeling of not being as loved as much as before. At least before you felt a sense of security. But now, you are not sure.

From time to time during the first few days you may find yourself angry at the custodial parent—the parent who didn't leave. You may have all sorts of emotions. You may feel cheated or lonely. You will certainly feel like neither parent has done what you wanted. You may even want to run away but you realize it would only make matters worse. This is something from which you cannot run. Like overeating, running away is a poor solution.

How do you handle this resentment, this anger? How do you get over the emptiness that has taken over? When will the house seem right again?

Getting over the emptiness of a missing parent will be difficult, no matter how brave you are. Even if the other parent tries to make it seem *okay,* you will still find it hard to understand. The fact remains that one of your parents is living somewhere else.

Of course that is part of the way you will adjust to the loneliness of the missing parent. Remember that parent will soon have a different address. That parent doesn't have to be missing for very long. Just as soon as you get the right telephone number or address, you can make contact. That person doesn't have the same address as you, that person's clothes and personal items are gone, but you are not truly apart. You are just living at different places. You can connect.

Just as soon as you know that the away parent is okay, has a new address, a phone, a place to watch television and to go on with daily chores, you will be able to handle the emptiness of the house. Perhaps you actually helped this parent settle into an apartment or house. The child who is made a part of the move is generally more content and less disturbed by the change. The old house won't seem so strange, so empty. You can see the parent in the new apartment or house and know that he or she is okay. You can ask to help in making the move.

When you stop to think about it, it is not so much of a concern that the parent is gone, but how that parent is getting along. How's that parent doing? Are things starting to work out for that parent? Actually, that's what you really want to know. And, as soon as you feel that your parent is safe and well, you'll be all right.

> *It is not so much of a concern that the parent is gone, but how that parent is getting along.*

Just as every person is unique, each family member will be affected differently in a divorce situation. The little ones, of course, will not fully understand the emptiness of the house. They will simply wonder what is going to happen next.

As for you, it's actually up to you now. Try to remember that things change. It's up to you how soon you become your old self again. It's up to you how soon you return to normal and let the adults go ahead and do what they feel they must do.

At some point you will return to the *old* you, doing pretty much what you used to do—enjoying the same tapes, the same CDs, hanging out with or writing to the same friends, and getting along with both of your parents. You won't really like the new arrangement too much at first, but you can cope with it. As soon as possible, try to visit the away parent. You'll feel better.

There's something else that is up to you. If, by any chance, you are blaming yourself because your parents are getting a divorce, forget it. It just isn't so. No child is to blame for their parents splitting up and you must stop thinking that way immediately. You may have disobeyed them, you may have been rude, too mouthy, and you may have even caused your parents to quarrel about something that happened, but you are not to blame for their divorce. You have enough to think about without taking unnecessary blame.

Of course, you should be sorry that you disobeyed, or that you were rude, but your actions did not cause the divorce. Your parents made the decision. The adults are getting this divorce for their own reasons, not because of something you did or did not do.

Remember, when two parents make a good home and treat each other and the family members with kindness, there is nothing a child can do to cause a divorce. It simply cannot be done.

If either parent is blaming you, then that parent is wrong, confused, and not being very mature. Parents have a right to get a divorce, but they do not have a right to blame their children. They are not being fair or honest if they blame anyone but themselves.

Chapter 7
Changes and Money

There will be some other changes in your life that you can't do anything about except to be fair, decent, and reasonable. In a remarkably short time, for instance, your parents, who used to do things together, now have a different set of friends.

Most of those *old* friends are in the same situation as you. They are not exactly sure how and where they fit in the picture. Your friends may not change, but chances are, your parents' friends will.

More than likely both of your parents will find new friends. Along with a few old regulars, there may be several new friends. There may be friends of the opposite sex. This will be a great change for you. It may not happen right away, but you need to be ready to meet the new people that come into your parents' lives. You may be quite surprised by the many new people and friends that come into the picture.

> *Money or the shortage of it may have helped bring on the divorce.*

Another change may involve money or the shortage of it. All too often there is less income, at least at first. It is possible that your parents really hadn't considered all the extra expenses of running two homes. Money or the lack of it may become a serious problem.

Money or the shortage of it may have helped bring on the divorce. If one parent was wasting and squandering too much of the money and it wasn't being spent on the family, then the custodial parent may have more money to spend on groceries and family expenses after the divorce. Your primary family may be better off financially.

That might be a change for the better. At least one of your parents could be in a better situation. The custodial parent may be able to budget—work things out better than before.

However, a shortage of money may force that parent to find a job, or change jobs, or go to work full-time. You may have a sitter. You, especially if you are the eldest sibling, may have to watch the little ones more often. Perhaps you will become a "latchkey" child. Perhaps you were a latchkey child even before the divorce. That means you had a key to the house and let yourself in. Being a latchkey child means that you have to be extremely responsible—use your head. It is a time when really good children find it easy to get into trouble. You have to be strong!

The shortage of money is a serious problem, but not one that you can't overcome. If the lack of money has always been a problem and it is even worse now that your parents have separated, there are service agencies, food stamps, welfare, and government housing departments that will make sure you and your family survive. Your family will be okay. The family will make it no matter how bad it may seem to you now.

If you or your custodial parent is unsure as to how to go about getting some of these services that are available, your school counselor, teacher, or religious leader can advise you. There are many, many programs to help the truly needy, but your custodial parent will have to seek them out. You may be able to help by supplying proper phone numbers. The telephone directory can be very confusing. The librarian can look up the numbers in the phone book to help you. Agencies often have strange names, but with determination, you can find the proper place to call.

This new shortage of money, if there is one, does not have to change your plans for college or technical school. There are many grants and other funds for low income students. Keep your grades up as much as you can and keep your attendance high to show that you are a responsible person. You won't have to worry in later years, even if money is tight at the moment.

Every student, rich or poor, cheats himself or herself if a good school record is not an important part of life. Your school record follows you for years. It will be on job applications, resumes, college applications, military applications, and more.

Get the best record possible. If you have not done well in the past, it is not too late to begin now. You can quickly overcome a poor junior high or middle school record. If you are a freshman with a poor school record, your next two or three years can help bring it into a satisfactory record. Future employers look to the final years more than the early years. Most employers understand that growing up in today's world is tough and will overlook some problems on a school record. Just do your best.

Money may not be a problem. In many cases it is possible for the family to live just about as well as before the divorce. Child support, the money paid by the noncustodial parent to the other parent, may be enough income to permit the family to live comfortably. Perhaps child support and a better job makes money not a serious problem.

Sometimes a family may decide to live in a larger home with relatives, often the grandparents. Their home may be larger and it may help them by having their kinfolk with them. Often they can help watch the children, cook for the larger family, or take the children to practices, doctors, and other commitments. They are supportive of their loved ones.

Of course, it must not be one-sided. If relatives open their home to your family, and it is decided that they can be a big help to the family, then the family must also do its part. There will be many ways in which the young people can help their older family members. Grandparents are great support systems, but their help must be appreciated. They may need your help, too.

Regardless of the situation, in a few years you may want to get a part-time or summer job. The work experience that you gain as you add to the family income will become an important treasure in your later years. Such experiences may make you grow up a little faster than you wish, but many corporate executives, famous athletes, and other successful adults remember fondly the time they spent on their part-time jobs.

> *You must not take any job if it prevents you from getting your education.*

Working while you are in school does present problems. You are still a child. Your main goal must be to get an education or some career training. It may be that you simply can't hold a job and keep up your grades at the same time. You must consider that possibility. School *must* come first.

Baby sitting or yard work might be ways to pick up enough money for new clothes, school supplies, pizzas, and a few extras. Sitting with the elderly at night, tutoring for an hour or two, or some such short jobs may be all that is open to you while you are in school. Watch for such jobs if that's all you can handle while in school.

You must not take any job if it prevents you from getting your education. This is a temporary stage of your life—surviving your parents' divorce. Education is not temporary. It must be given all that you can give. Things will get better and you must not let your education suffer.

This is a time when you also must consider what is best for you. It's *not* selfish to plan for the future. You should start planning, whether there is a divorce or not. The divorce may just push you to plan a little earlier.

After the separation you may be required to do more of the household chores. You may be asked to watch the smaller children, do some of the cooking, make your own bed every day (without argument), clean your room often, do some laundry, and perhaps do some of the yard work. Not really so different from before, is it? Doesn't that sound a little like something you have heard before? You won't

> *After the separation you may be required to do more of the household chores.*

be asked to do more than you can handle. You can do it. Grit your teeth and get it done. Stop putting off your chores and duties. It's time to pitch in.

In a way some of the changes are sensible. You will not be as childish or immature as you were. You will have become more responsible. You will have a sense of pride in the knowledge that you can accomplish something, get it done, whatever is necessary. It's more of what you can do, achievement.

Actually, none of these demands will be more than you can handle. If you have to watch a little less television, play a few less video games, hang out a little less, change your schedule, it won't bring on the end of the world.

Most often, these changes have an *up* side. They are not all *doom and gloom.* They may shorten your youthful fun days to some extent, but you may have been well on your way to becoming a teenage or preteen *slob*. Now, because you are organized and understand what you are supposed to be doing, you are growing up. You are now accepting some responsibility and quickly becoming an adult. Interestingly enough, you are becoming a better family member than when the family was all in tact.

You may find that taking on more of the chores will give you higher self-esteem. You will gain a feeling of importance and confidence. You are needed. You are important. You are not just a *selfish* teenager. Having parents who are divorced does not make you less important. It often makes you more needed.

There are usually some other common changes that have to be faced. Early in the separation you may sometimes feel your parents are not concerned enough about you. Perhaps your *away* parent does not seem to have time for you. That person doesn't call. That person doesn't get in touch with you. This makes you feel alone and uneasy.

You must try to remember that it takes time for your non-custodial parent to find a new home. If it is an apartment or house, it has to be furnished. Maybe that person is living in a motel for a while. It is difficult.

Actually, there is no excuse for a parent to ignore his or her children. It shouldn't happen. However, that person is no doubt filled with confusion, perhaps depression, perhaps fear. Even adults find themselves alone with their problems at times. Sometimes they can't make themselves do a difficult chore. Just having to *call* the children may send them into a panic. Parents often are afraid to face problems.

Fortunately, these things usually work out relatively quickly. Your parents are not deliberately trying to ignore or hurt you.

They are probably just covered up with changes of their own. That makes it impossible for them to do the right thing, face the people they are hurting most—their children.

Sometimes a new person, a girl friend or boy friend, has taken up with the away parent. Often, that parent is too busy carving out a new life to remember the pain in the child. Adults get lonely, too. They do reach out for members of the opposite sex. They seem to need some time to get over their fears. They seem to need company and friendship, especially if they are going through a mid-life crisis (the time when they see their life passing by too soon).

Why not get on with your own responsibilities and give everyone—including yourself—some space? It is short termed. Your parent will come around. When the noncustodial parent gets an address, a phone number, and gets somewhat settled in, he or she will get in touch. You can count on it. The contact with the missing parent may take longer than it should, but you will eventually hear from that person.

There will be times when you will feel sorry for yourself. It is true that parents should make every effort not to disappoint you. Yet, they do. The problem is that they are also struggling with their emotions. They may not be thinking straight. They may ignore you, say the wrong things, even hurt you with their actions, but this is only for a short while.

It might help if you would tell them that you are feeling a little left out. Explain your feelings whenever you can. It is a real loss if the members of the family stop talking to each other or stop listening. Don't let this happen if you can help it. Keep the lines open. This really is the parents' responsibility, but you have done some "parenting" already. You know all about that.

Occasionally, you may become disgusted and overwhelmed. You may *want* to be alone. You may not want to talk with friends. You may be angry. You may be mad. Sometimes you won't know exactly what it is that you want or expect from your parents. The fog will lift in time. Just give yourself a break and don't be too hard on yourself.

Often people expect more from you than you can give. You are going to make mistakes, get angry at times, and become difficult. You will soon learn, however, to take each day at as it comes and you will find fewer and fewer times when you are angry.

> *You are not going to be able to please everyone in this confused world.*

You are not going to be able to please everyone in this confused world, no matter how well you are holding up. You aren't going to be the perfect example of a well-adjusted child coping well with problems. No one is perfect.

You will shake the blues as you become drawn to your own activities and less concerned about the changes in your life. You will concentrate more on the future and less on the past. You will adjust a little each day.

Someday, in the not too distant future, you are going to enter the job market full time with a regular paycheck. You can make your present situation a learning experience. In other words, as you build your own life, you will learn from your parents' divorce. Their actions may affect the kind of life you want to give to your own children. It may make you understand the importance of making wise decisions now and through the years.

Much of your future happiness will depend on your own attitude. If you insist on being unhappy and resentful, you can be fairly sure that you can remain quite miserable. On the other hand, if you make a real effort to set aside your gloom and strive to make the best of your situation, you will be taking charge of a very important thing, your own life.

Learning to be responsible, making it possible for people to count on you, making your word good, and doing what is expected and necessary is character building. It is a part of growing up, developing a philosophy, and determining what kind of an adult you want to be.

You will soon find that being a mature child isn't so bad. You may be young now, but the years will fly by and you will be in charge of your life. You will be respected and feel good about yourself. You will remember the painful divorce, but it will be simply a memory, a memory that doesn't hurt so much anymore.

You need to remember that there are people who care, that your parents love you, and that changes and disappointments are common to everyone. Build your goals, develop your personality positively, and do not settle for being less than you can be. It really is up to you.

Chapter 8
Staying Out of the Middle

One of the most serious problems you are likely to face is that of staying out of your parents' quarrels. All too often, in their rush to prove that they are doing the right thing in getting a divorce, they will try to involve you in their arguments. They will sometimes insist that you take sides, agree with one of them, turn against the other.

Sometimes one or both parents will put you right in the middle of their heated debates. Hopefully, this won't happen to you because it is cruel. At times it could even be dangerous.

Parents are wrong when they make you take sides, or try to get you to say mean things about the other parent. Even if one parent is clearly more to blame than the other, you, as a child in the family, already know it. It won't help by getting you into the battle. It hurts if you are asked to drag one parent through the mud—say cruel things—whether it is deserved or not.

Taking sides cannot do any good. It only makes matters worse. When parents hate each other, the children should be allowed to remain as neutral as possible. You must find ways to stay out of it.

Taking sides adds to the pain and hurt of the other siblings as well. The younger children have no idea how to deal with this terrible kind of pressure coming from the people they love.

You and your brothers and sisters, if there are any, have bonded to your parents—both parents. That means these two people have been the primary members in your family. There may be others who have been important or significant, but your mother and father are the two people who have managed the household, made decisions, and have brought good and bad memories to you for a long time. Now they are enemies.

One parent may be lazy, unpleasant, disappointing, and disgusting, but still there has been an attachment—a bonding. This person is still a member of the family. The children can't help it if that parent is less than he or she should be. The children shouldn't be forced into making any nasty comments. They shouldn't be forced to take sides.

Bonding is unbelievably powerful. Children will cling to the most unkind and unworthy loved one against all odds. A child will often prefer to stay with an abusive parent rather than hurt that cruel, unkind parent. Such children have learned to love that parent and have become deeply attached to that person, good or bad.

Even if the child realizes that one parent is not the kind of role model he or she should be, it is painful to admit such a thing, especially during an argument between parents. It is usually painful for the child to even admit such a thing to himself or herself.

> *The parent who forces you to take sides in such emotional moments is wrong.*

Even if the child is going to be very glad to get that person out of the house, it doesn't help for the child to have to say hateful things about that parent. There will be plenty of time to decide who is right and who is wrong. Even if the household will be better off and the future will be brighter when the parents have separated and one parent has left, no real good can come from a child being made to openly talk about the evil side of his mother or father. Don't do it. Don't let a parent make you do it.

If you are in such a situation, and many children are, it will help if you realize exactly what is happening. You must understand that the parent who forces you to take sides in such emotional moments is wrong. Involving you and trying to make you enter into the fighting is wrong. This parent is trying to make you and/or the other children become as emotional as he or she is. The parent is being totally unfair.

Of course, it is difficult not to enter into the argument and try to help one parent over the other, but you must stay out of it. Words spoken cruelly are not easily forgotten.

Even if you feel sorry for one of them and you very much want to sympathize with one parent, be careful. Things are bad enough already.

Fortunately, there are some ways to stay out of the middle. It's a stressful situation and you have to be careful, but you can do it. You can get out of and keep out of the middle by knowing what to say, how to answer, and by keeping your own wits about you.

> *You can come up with some suitable answers that will actually get you out of their arguments.*

The secret is partly in how you answer. You must give reasonable replies. Actually, if you were to refuse to answer, if you didn't criticize that person, you would seem to be disobedient. This hateful or bad action won't help you.

Yet, when asked for your opinion, a true and honest response could not only get you in trouble but it would hurt the very person you don't want to hurt. You must answer wisely, especially if the parent is demanding an answer. You must find a way to squirm out of this trapped position.

It may sound like an impossible situation, but it is not. You can come up with some suitable answers that will actually get you out of their arguments—their quarrels. It is possible that the right answer might even be able to quiet the two sides— calm them down. That must be your goal as your parents fight with each other and try to get you to fight with them. It's more of that parenting job you seem to be taking on, using better judgment than your parents. You should be getting pretty good at it by now.

The following chapter will give you a head start on planning your answers. Try to learn the ones that seem to fit your situation. Remember, all families are different, but you are learning to understand what works for you and your family.

Learn the responses so well that you can say them easily. Make up some of your own and practice. You will do much better if you give a calming, sensible answer. Practice it so that it comes out of your mouth politely. Politeness and tone of voice are important keys.

You become a referee of sorts. Such parenting, which you may already be somewhat of an expert, is wise. Remember, parenting is the act of taking care of your parents. That's what you would be doing by keeping calm and helping them to keep calm.

Go to your room, or the family desk, and get some paper, a small notebook, something upon which to write and study suitable replies. Take this positive step now. It will make you feel better and it will help you out of a difficult corner.

Educational Media Corporation®

Chapter 9
Some Good Answers

What are some good answers to the questions people often ask? What should you say to your parents? When should you say it? How should you say it? And, what shouldn't you say? Let's take some common situations and make up some replies.

Suppose your mother is upset with your father because he has come home again in a drunken state. Your father is loud and ready to fight. She is extremely upset and wants some help. She has started quarreling with your father and you understand fully why she is angry. You feel a little sorry, maybe very sorry, for her since this is not the first time. You've seen it before. You are disgusted, too. You really want to help. You feel you should get involved. Your father does have a drinking problem.

Then your mother looks directly at you and says, "See what I have to put up with?" She naturally wants you to say, "Yes, he's wrong." She may want you to tell your father that you agree with her, that he should not come home drunk. He should not spend the grocery money on booze.

Of course, in this case, your mother is correct. Dad should not come home drunk. He should not come home and pick a fight. But then, you realize that he came home after having been drinking, but he did not really start the quarrel. It seemed to you that he wanted to go to bed. He needed to sleep it off.

If you were to say something to support your mother, something like, "Dad, why are you doing this to Mother?" you have entered into the war zone. Now, anything you say will more than likely just make matters worse. Then, with what your mother and father will add, the argument will grow. You will have become part of the enemy even though you just wanted to help. Be careful, words can cause violence.

Then what happens? The combat zone with two very emotional people, one of which is drunk and one is emotional, now has three people arguing. There may be even more than three if other children are in the room. Is this in the best interest of the family? It has become a family feud. Nothing is solved, even for the moment.

Was your mother correct in mentioning something about your father's drinking habits? Probably, she couldn't help it. She was extremely upset and truly wanted some support. Unfortunately, she doesn't realize that you can't argue with someone who is extremely emotional or extremely intoxicated.

Your mother is right in some ways. She may have been worrying about it for a long time, but no one can help the situation when everyone is so upset. You feel sorry for her. You hate to see your father *drunk and mean again*. What can you say to make things better? You must answer wisely.

In this particular situation, with two of your loved ones quarreling, you can argue, fight, punch, ridicule, criticize, beg, and nag, but you can't win. A person in a drunken state is in no condition to talk sensibly. That person can't think straight.

> **Be careful, words can cause violence.**

Often, they appear quite sane and rational, but they are always too drunk to make wise decisions. This is true of an emotional person as well. Neither of them is likely to make sense in their statements. They are out of it. What do you do?

Here's where a good answer might help. You, with your quick wit and great wisdom, could make a difference. You could turn to your mother and say, "Let's see if we can get Dad to go to bed now and talk about this in the morning. Mom, you need to get some rest, too." What a nice, polite, and neutral answer from a child trying to avoid more trouble.

With this response you have stayed out of it quite nicely and still comforted your mother. Your father may not be completely willing to go to bed, but encouraging him to kick off his shoes can't add much fuel to the stormy situation.

Or you could say to your mother, "I don't think we can solve this drinking problem tonight while there is so much anger in the air. Let's wait until we all feel better."

Certainly you get the idea. You can decide how far you can go. Maybe you can actually help your father to bed and put your arm around your mother as you go back to her. If you study the problems, you can find other good answers and actions.

Remember that you have to be thinking about this and practicing your lines if this is a regular occurrence at your house. And you have to be willing to do it.

Let us take another example. Suppose you want to side with your father. Perhaps your mother is a disappointment. She doesn't seem to take good care of the children, the house is a mess, or she doesn't like cooking and won't cook for her family. Your father is upset. They are getting a divorce. They are fighting as usual. Your dad may say something hurtful like, "Just look at your son (or daughter). You're an unfit mother. I'll be glad when you are out of here. I can take better care of these children than you ever could."

Then, he adds, looking right at you, "Isn't that true, child? How do you like the way your mom washes your clothes? She's no good." Such a comment is extremely hurtful. He may call your mother many other nasty names. You simply don't have words to express how sad the whole thing makes you feel. In some ways what your dad is saying is true, but he should not force you into a hurtful remark.

In this case you can probably get away with simply not answering at all. Your dad may be just exploding, trying to get rid of his frustration and his worries. He just may be thinking out loud. You probably won't have to enter into the issue. Let the distressed parent go on and on. Maybe a reply isn't necessary.

But, what if he insists that you agree with him? You know that much of what he says is true. Your mother doesn't seem to care about anything anymore. What can you answer?

One suitable answer to not hurt either person might be, "Dad, I understand what you are saying, but I don't know what to say or do about it. I have to leave all these problems up to you and Mom."

Whenever you are forced to answer a person who is becoming violent, get away.

That's not the answer your father wanted, but it will usually work. If you are forced to answer again, you can say, "I'm too confused to make a decision. Please don't ask me." You could say, "I don't know what's right or wrong. I just want the two of you to work this out. I want the best for the both of you."

Whenever you are forced to answer a person who is becoming violent, or near the point of hurting someone, get away. Go to the bathroom, the porch, or the kitchen. Hopefully the anger will pass and you will be safe.

You can see how the following statements will help you stay out of the middle in any number of situations. Start or end your comments with, "I'm not sure what to do about..."

or "I wish I could help but I'm too confused to..." or

"Perhaps we need to get some professional help about..."

or "Let me think about this until...."

There's nothing wrong with saying very firmly but kindly, "I don't want to get into this argument." Or, "I wish I had a way to make this problem go away, but I can't." Better yet, it may be wise to simply ask if you could be permitted to leave the room. You could say, "I don't know what to say or do, may I leave the room?" Or you could say, "I need some time alone to think about our problems." Actually, you probably should have left the room before they had a chance to pin you down for an answer.

It seems that fear often enters the picture. When there is trouble brewing, many children stick around to see if they can help one parent or the other. One parent may seem to be in danger. If you feel you shouldn't leave, then be very careful to stay out of the quarrel.

Also, the tone you use when making your statements is very important. If you always answer calmly and politely, your parents will have *no* reason to be angry with you. In time they may learn that you always have a soft, neutral answer, and maybe it will make them see how disgusting their family quarrels are. They will probably quit trying to involve you when they don't get the support and comfort they are seeking.

In the meantime, you will feel better because you used your head and did not let their fights become your fights. Later, you may want to go to one or both of your parents when they are alone and express your fears and concerns, but not in the heat of the battle. You love both of them. You have bonded with both. You don't want to hurt either of them, and by staying out of the middle, you have helped them both whether they know it or not.

Sometimes it is possible to go a step further, beyond a soft answer. For instance, you may fully realize that one parent is absolutely right and the other is quite wrong. When you are alone with the parent who is obviously more at fault than the other, you may be able to do some more parenting. You may be able to say, "Mom, I feel you need some help. What can I do? Do you want to get better?" She may just be waiting for a chance to get some help.

You may want to offer to do a little extra around the house. It might help if you did your chores a little more willingly. You can ask, "Mom, would it help if I took the baby outside?" "Dad, is there anything I can do at this time to help?"

Just do what you can do and remember that things always change.

Remember, parenting is not your job. You would simply be trying to be a good family member, but you won't regret any effort you make. It won't hurt to try.

Chances are that all of your efforts will fail. Nothing you do or say helps one bit. Even so, by developing and using classic, kind answers and offering to help, you are doing a great deal, certainly more than the quarreling parents are doing.

Don't blame yourself. Just do what you can do and remember that things always change. The unpleasantness will not go on forever. They are getting a divorce and you will handle the other problems as they arise. You have done your best and it's a good feeling. You are determined to get through this mess. You are a survivor.

Start today on your list of perfect answers. You can let a close friend or relative help you put the words into a simple reply. Ask them, " What should I say when...?" It's going to take a of lot of studying. It's hard to respond to insults about an affair, personal habits, drugs, or any of the problems your family may be suffering. Think it through, make up some suitable answers, and practice them in case you need them.

Who knows, you could even ask your parents what to answer when the other parent is trying to involve you. Ask one parent at a time, "Mom (Dad), what can I say when (the other parent) tries to get me to say something bad about you?" It may make your parents understand how disturbing their actions are. It's another way of communicating, getting the message across.

Chapter 10
Custody

As the divorce action continues, there is another subject that becomes very important to both you and your parents. One of the key issues your parents have to decide is, "Who gets the children?" Or more aptly stated, "With whom will the children live?" This is the question of custody.

Usually, you will live with one parent more than the other. This parent is said to have "custody" and is referred to as the "custodial" parent. The other parent, the one with whom you will not live every day, is called the "noncustodial" parent. That doesn't mean you won't see your noncustodial parent. It merely means that you will make your primary, or main, home with the custodial parent while the other parent picks you up on certain holidays, weekends, or whatever days have been chosen.

There have been many battles over who gets the children. Often it is a fairly simple question for the parents to answer. More often than not the children stay with their mother. Usually parents agree rather easily. Other times, they battle it out.

Even so, custody is not an automatic placement. Several things have to be considered. For instance, are the children very young? Are the children old enough to decide with which parent they wish to live? Will one parent have a great deal more income? Is income important? Is one parent unfit or unable to raise the children? Is one parent ill? Will one parent have other relatives to help in the rearing of the children? All these are important factors in deciding where the children will live.

When the custody decision is finally made, you will usually live with one parent and that parent will provide your primary home. You will, of course, visit the noncustodial parent as often as conveniently possible. This noncustodial parent may not see you as much as before, but you may be sure that both parents want what is best for you and will stand ready to help you whenever you need it.

Educational Media Corporation®

Most often the parents have decided earlier who gets the children—with whom will they live—but not always. In a bitter divorce, it is sometimes necessary for the courts to make the decision. Once in a while, according to your age and needs, the judge will let you chose with which parent you would like to live.

Although it is not a common practice, your custodial person or guardian could be a grandparent. It can be an older family member if conditions are right.

If a judge does help in the choice, you may be sure that your welfare will be the primary concern. The judge tries to take everything into consideration. You, or the other children, will not be left out of the judge's thinking.

Caring parents will try to make custody arrangements go smoothly.

If you find yourself in one of those rare situations where you are placed in a custody arrangement that is very much against your wishes, remember it is not forever. Your case can be taken back to the courts later on when you are older.

In any case you should continue to do the best you can in school or sports so that when it is time for you to have a say concerning your custody, you will have proven that you can make good decisions.

Caring parents will try to make custody arrangements go smoothly. When the children are comfortable and adjusted in a particular school, the parents tend to keep their children in the same school. That means the children have the same home, same bedroom, same friends, same family pet, same car, same church, same neighbors, and even the same mail person. It does not become a total change.

In such a case the noncustodial parent, the one who no longer lives in your primary home, finds an apartment or another house and sets up a home. That home then becomes a second home to you. You can visit, stay overnight, and explore the new environment. Hopefully you will feel welcome and loved in both homes.

It may seem overwhelming to you right now, but it need not be. That first night in your new second home can be exciting, different, and quite interesting. There are new children to meet, new places to go, and new experiences.

It will be different, but it can be a very happy, pleasant time. You and your noncustodial parent may find this new arrangement brings both of you closer. You may find it easier to show your love when the parents have gone their separate ways.

Sometimes it takes a real adjustment, but nothing a normal child can't handle. For instance, perhaps your second home is a one bedroom apartment. You may sleep on the couch or in a sleeping bag. That is not such a bad thing, especially if you get the living room and the television remote is right beside you. If you can keep a good, helpful, considerate attitude, it will help this parent settle in more easily, even if it is in a motel room.

It is more difficult if your noncustodial parent moves away to another city or state. It will still be your second home, but visiting this parent may not be as often as you expected. In this situation you simply must go along with the decision. You will have to try to understand why the parent is not living close enough to permit you to visit often.

There could be many reasons for the noncustodial parent to move some distance from the custodial parent. Perhaps the divorce required a job change and a move to a distant city. Sometimes the noncustodial parent is moving in with friends for a while and the friends are in another town. Maybe the parents are so angry that they don't want to live in the same town.

This kind of reasoning is not completely fair to the children. The parents should be able to live in the same town together and share the children, but there may be circumstances of which you are not aware. There may be valid reasons for them to live a distance apart.

> *Hopefully you will be kind to both parents, wherever they live.*

Remember, even if you are unhappy with the arrangement, things will change. Nothing stays the same. You will learn patience. Hopefully you will be kind to both parents, wherever they live.

There is another custody option that families can consider. When both parents live near each other and want to share you more equally, they set up "joint custody" or "co-custody." You are permitted to stay at both of their homes on a more regular basis.

This can be a good choice of custody since it doesn't interfere with the children going to the same school, playing on the same teams, belonging to the same clubs, and participating in activities. With joint custody, the children have extra clothes, books, games, and other important things at both homes. They are *free* to go back and forth between the two parents' homes.

It can work out fine if the parents agree. It works well only if the parents are willing to make it work. Sometimes they disagree so deeply that joint custody is out of the question.

Sometimes it is difficult for the parents to agree on how much child support will be provided to one parent from the other when they are sharing equal custody. Sometimes it is left to the courts, the lawyers, and the judges.

Parents are often so emotional about the whole thing that they don't want to share you at all. In other words, they are fighting over you. As the days go by they may change, but in this case they are determined to have it their way. Remember, they are in a terrible state of change themselves. It may take time for them to solve the many problems they have to face before they are able to make other decisions.

You, as a child, can't insist on where you will or will not live. You must do as your parents or the courts decide. You must try to make the best of it until your custody changes for some reason or another, such as your age or your parents' situation. It could be that one parent will have to prove that he or she is a *good* parent before custody changes.

The main thing to consider is your own attitude. Whatever card is dealt to you, whether you like it or not, you won't help the situation if you are mean and hateful. You won't be a good family member if you deliberately cause problems and make it difficult for your parents. You must help the family by being as fair as possible, even when it is hard to do, even when it doesn't seem fair.

It is extremely important that you continue to be involved with your school activities, your sports, your clubs, and your friends. Your mental outlook will be healthier, your days will be fuller and more pleasant, and the future will be brighter.

If for some reason you have to move away to a different city and school, it is best if you get involved as soon as possible. You must try to settle down in your new nest, your new town, and get on with your life.

You will still graduate, still find fun places to go, nice people to meet, and churches, libraries, stores, video shops, and other things that are important to

> *It is extremely important that you continue to be involved with your school activities.*

you. Give yourself a chance. Under the worst of circumstances, you will still have a home (actually two), still have a chance at a good education, and still live amongst friends.

Many children of divorce have discovered that having parents living in two places is not so bad when all is said and done. They get attention from both parents, go different places, do different things, and actually find some extra enjoyment through the arrangement.

Of course it's probably not as good as having the nice, comfortable, original family, but it is possible to enjoy the new situation. You may eventually learn to like it, especially at Christmas and your birthdays. You may have friends that will tell you the same thing. You may have many friends whose parents are living apart.

Educational Media Corporation®

You may be angry at times, lonely, and even hateful, but as you work through it, you will see yourself growing up quickly, wiser, and ready to face any new challenge that comes your way. Try to be patient with your parents. They love you and will continue to love you throughout their lifetime.

They will make mistakes, but that is part of living. It's only a matter of time until you will be old enough to make major decisions on your own. That can be scary, too. Hopefully, as you grow in years and wisdom, you won't make too many mistakes.

Chapter 11
The Far, Far Away Parent

Up until now you may have handled the divorce with a fair amount of control. You may have worked through all the changes that were created by the divorce. You may have even kept your spirits up when one parent moved out of the house. Now, suppose you receive some startling news. You learn that your non-custodial parent is moving across the country—far, far away.

It will take a whole new set of plans to deal with such a discouraging problem. It might even take you several days to realize that your parent is going to be living a long distance away. However, when you finally begin to deal with this knowledge, you also will begin to make plans that will satisfy both you and your far, far away parent.

First you must remember this parent is probably as concerned about this move as you are. This parent, no doubt, has fears just as you do. It is probably extremely troubling that he or she will be miles and miles away from you.

> *Both parents will want to be a part of your life, whether they live far away or not.*

Naturally you will visit this far away parent. Perhaps not as often as either of you would like, but you will probably have longer visits. Both parents will want to be a part of your life, whether they live far away or not. They will want to watch you grow up. They will want you to turn to them when you need them.

As soon as possible you need to have a serious talk with the parent who is moving away. It can be a very rewarding experience for the two of you. This serious talk will give you an opportunity to talk over the good and bad features of this parent having to move away. You can make plans together, discussing how you are going to deal with visiting each other.

You must try to discuss the move in as reasonable fashion as possible. Ask your parent such questions as, "How soon will I be able to visit you?" Or, "How often will I be allowed to visit?" "Will I spend two or three months of my summer vacation with you?"

Find out if you will be able to spend a whole summer with this parent if you want to do so.

Maybe you won't want to leave your primary home for a long visit with the away parent. That's something you need to talk about, if possible, before the parent leaves. You will find that you can deal with this change if you know in advance what to expect. Your parents need to understand that.

Discuss the holidays. Will you be spending two weeks at Christmas? Will you visit during spring break? How will you get there? Get out an atlas and figure out the route, the many ways you can get to your new second home. The main thing is to communicate with this far away person before he or she has moved away.

Plan to use the telephone. Ask your parent how often you may call. Children soon learn that the telephone is a most delightful way to keep in touch with away parents. This parent may be out of the city but not so far away that there is no telephone service. That parent won't be living in a jungle or an Alaskan outpost.

If telephoning becomes too expensive, one of the best ways to let the parent who has moved away know about you is by writing. You can write about what you are doing, how you are doing, how you are feeling, and when you will be visiting again. You may even be able to write some letters on a computer. Children are getting pretty good at using word processors. Your progress on learning the computer would be very interesting to the far away parent. You may want to use e-mail.

If you are old enough to do the math required, you could probably figure out a *bargain* long distance service. It's a tricky business, but your parents can help you choose the most inexpensive way to call long distance. They will do this for you. They will help you.

Telephoning is nice, but there are some good reasons for writing besides just keeping in touch. It's a good way to get things off your mind and share important things. You can even keep copies of your letters. You will enjoy reading them later. Writing to your parent can be like keeping a journal. You can explain your deepest feelings and fears in a letter. Tell of the good and the bad. The far away parent wants to hear from you and it's good that you help to keep the channels open. Keeping in touch is very, very important and you can help make it happen.

A letter from you will be a welcome communication. It may cause a teardrop or two when the parent finds a letter from you, but it will be a very welcome letter when he or she comes home from work some evening—tired and weary. It can be a pleasant surprise. Finding such a letter from a son or daughter will be a comfort, bring a warm smile after the tears. You can do that. You will be proud if you comfort or bring a smile to the face of your away parent. You are still bonding and not letting the ties break.

Children often find that the away parent actually keeps all those notes and letters that they receive. You, too, will probably save the letters you receive from your far away parent.

There is another thing to consider. It may be that every letter you write is not answered right away. You may eagerly wait for a letter that doesn't arrive in a reasonable amount of time. It's a disappointment and you will begin to feel that your parent doesn't care about you, but that parent does love and care about you. That parent just isn't quite up to handling such emotions.

Actually, the problem is that sometimes adults just do not get around to writing letters like most children write notes. It seems natural for children to write long notes. That's not true of most parents unless they use a computer with a word processor.

Also, adults often put off doing things because they are too busy, unsure of what to say, or just too tired. You must guard against worrying about which of you is writing more than the other. You can be certain that your away parent welcomes your letters and phone calls.

What is important is that you continue to share your life with your far away parent. Picture in your mind your parent reading your words. Later on you may be the one who is too busy with a job, sports, or friends to write as often as before. Never let it become a counting match. Don't sit around waiting for an answer if you feel like writing. Go ahead and write. Keep in touch.

> *What is important is that you continue to share your life with your far away parent.*

If you are an older brother or sister, you may want to include small messages written by your younger siblings. Little children can scribble on a piece of paper and let you mail it. They can draw pictures. They can even put on the stamp. This can be very important to the away parent.

It can be something that you do regularly. You can make it a family tradition. With the younger ones, you can say, "Let's get a letter off to Dad (or Mom)." Your little siblings may remember those times fondly. They will love you all the more for those moments, for the family tradition you have helped make possible. You helped make the separation of your parents a bit easier to take.

It can be a way for the family to show love and it would mean a great deal to the far away parent. You will be taking a big step in helping the family mend and keeping the younger children in touch.

There is no question but that divorce can be a very difficult situation, but you must understand that you are not losing a parent. You are still a family and you still love each other. Even if weeks go by without a word from the away parent, that person is still your parent. You may have to be the one who keeps the door open for awhile , but in time, hopefully that parent will soon be back on track and answering more promptly.

So you must not be too alarmed if your parent has moved far away. Members may go in and out of a particular location from time to time, but they are still members of the family.

Older brothers and sisters may get married and have their own immediate families, but they are still part of the original family. Things change everyday, but family is still family.

You are not walking away from them.

It does not have to be a family full of stress. By knowing what to expect and accepting these changes, you can actually play an important part in making the changes easier for everyone. You can, indeed, be the key to helping keep your family a family.

Chapter 12
New Adults in Your Life

Somewhere along the way, maybe even before you are ready for more changes, you may face another troubling situation. You may have been doing well, adjusting to a new house, making friends in school, and meeting the events of each day without fear. Then, quite without warning, you meet another new problem, a somewhat confusing challenge. A new adult enters the scene.

This mysterious person may be a new friend of your mother or your father. This person may not even be a stranger. This person could be someone that one or both of your parents knew. Only this time it's different. There's something strange about this person. You are a little suspicious, curious.

In any case, this person appears to be a rather nice person, but something makes you not fully trust any new adult that comes into the family picture. You find yourself looking this person over very carefully, studying him or her very closely. Is this person as nice as he or she appears or is the person just pretending? Here are some possible situations.

Suppose it is a new friend of your mother's that has entered into the picture. Soon this friend begins to take your mother out to dinner or a movie. Or perhaps you mom begins to prepare a dinner at your house and this person is invited. This person seems to enjoy being with the family.

You are a little uneasy about having this guest at your table. You were just getting used to the new family—the changed family. Now there is another person. That person may be sitting at the same place at the table where your away parent used to sit. You have a strange feeling about it.

Perhaps this person rents a video and your mom makes some popcorn. Everyone watches the show together. It looks a little like a family. You may like the idea of having company, but for some reason you resent the attention being shown to your mom. As you study this situation, you may frown from time to time.

Your mom seems to enjoy all this fun they are having. She seems to be watching you, trying to understand what you are thinking.

In fact, you may be a little jealous. That's quite possible. It's not surprising. You have been doing your part to help keep this family happy, adjusted, and together. Once again questions and doubts race through your mind. Why is this couple so comfortable together? Is it okay? Should you be angry? Should you want your parents to make new friends? Did that person touch your mom? Were they acting too friendly? When will this person go home? After you have gone to bed, will he kiss her? How did you feel about it?

The question haunts you, "How is this new person going to change the family?" Are you, for instance, looking at a possible stepparent? Why? What about your other parent? Is this new person a threat?

Each person you meet and each new friend you make changes your life to some degree.

This new person and everyone else that you meet will affect your life in some way. This person might even cause another big change. Of course, you should have some doubts and questions about how it's going to affect you. You have a right to frown and be a bit slow in checking out this person. That's quite natural.

Each person you meet and each new friend you make changes your life to some degree. That's one strong reason that everyone should choose their friends wisely. Our peers *do* affect us differently. Hopefully, your parent does not jump too fast into a new lifestyle.

Chances are at this point your mom is simply trying to get past the pain and get started on a new, hopefully better life. This person and your mom may simply be getting acquainted just like anyone else.

Actually a new friend might just be what your mom or other parent needs to get back to living normally. She may have felt that she wanted to get out of the house, go somewhere, do something different. Their relationship may come to nothing more than a much needed friendship or a night out.

Or you may find that your dad has just found a girlfriend and you are expected to meet her, go to dinner, and be nice. Of course you will go and you will be nice. You cannot do anything other than be a decent child in a pleasant or troublesome encounter.

However, what if you feel she is not suitable for your father? You are making an early judgement. Are you supposed to be polite and well mannered? Of course. It must be important to your father or you wouldn't have been invited to go with them. Something is happening.

More questions come to you. How should you feel about any of these new strangers (or old friends) that come into your parents' lives and appear to be taking over, or fitting into the family circle? Is it normal to be resentful, jealous, and somewhat angry? Of course. Do you have to be nice when you really want to complain? No, you don't have to be pleasant, but how does it benefit you or anyone else to be hateful and moody?

Look at it this way. Just as you got used to the idea that your parents were getting a divorce, you now will have to get used to the new people that come into your parents' lives. You will be looking at this situation with the same mixed emotions, not being sure exactly how you feel. At times it may seem quite disgusting that they wanted a divorce and now they want new people, too.

Once again, you are going to have to give yourself time to consider this new change. You need time to sort out your feelings. Don't panic. You will put things in the right place when you have the facts. Don't jump to conclusions. Don't show your likes or dislikes too soon. Give them and yourself some space.

Soon you will come to realize that it is normal for your parents to want friends, to go places, and to do things. Just as it is usually more fun to share adventures with your friends, so it is with adults. Some things, like a beautiful sunrise, a quiet walk, and a winning point for the team need to be shared.

Your parents are making friends to avoid loneliness, looking for friends to share activities.

Your parents are making friends to avoid loneliness, looking for friends to share activities. Your parents may be trying to overcome fears, doubt, and even some guilt. Your parents may be looking for some help. Your parents want to think that you are okay with the divorce. Your parents want to think that you will like their new friends.

If the previous marriage had so many problems that the parents divorced, then surely your parents will be more cautious this second time around. This time there are children involved. Surely each of your parents will be careful—very, very careful—the second time around.

It would be great if the children could choose every new person that enters their parents' lives, but it does not work that way. Just as children have a way of picking their own friends, so do adults.

There may be several new people who start dating your parents. You might wish there were only one, maybe two. That's enough. It might start to alarm you, but it probably shouldn't. You wouldn't want either of them to take the first person who showed a little kindness and interest. Hopefully, your parent is using good judgement in choosing a new partner or friend, but again, it's not up to you.

It may actually be somewhat better for you when your parents begin choosing a steady friend. It is possible that your parents may seem more cheerful at times, a little more content, and a little happier than you've ever seen before. You probably wouldn't want to change that.

It's probably not wise to get too upset when new companions enter the picture. New people in your parents' lives may have some advantages. It may take some of the stress off of you. Just don't jump to conclusions too early. Wait for the facts.

Maybe this new person is a further help by showing some real interest in the children in the family. Maybe you are getting to go more places. Maybe this person helps a little around the house. Maybe this person is truly fair and nice in dealing with you.

Continue to be as polite and cooperative as you know how to be. Good manners will be an asset, no matter what your parents decide. Nothing can be gained by your making unnecessary enemies, even if your feelings are a little hurt.

Of course, you are checking each person over to see if he or she would be a good or bad stepparent just in case the friendship turns to romance. Popcorn and video certainly gives you reason to think they are comfortable together. Are they serious about their relationship?

Is that bad? To be sure, Cinderella did have a very wicked stepmother and so did Snow White. Hansel and Gretel had scary problems, too. But these are fairy tales and not very happy ones until the end of the story.

Remembering these horror stories may set you to having some strange fears, but in the real world, it is seldom like that. Most stepparents contribute and make the new family stronger when given a fair chance.

More often than not the stepparent is not evil. This new person has fallen in love with your parent and hopefully wants to make the world right. Often this person truly wants to help you, to cooperate with you, and to make the situation better.

> *Should one of your parents start talking about remarriage, you may find yourself somewhat disappointed.*

If your parent does decide to remarry, both the parent and the friend, believe it is for the best. They have talked it over and want to make a more complete home for the family.

Should one of your parents start talking about remarriage, you may find yourself somewhat disappointed. You had probably thought that your parents would get back together. Now this talk of marriage has dashed your hopes. How should you react? What should you do? What's the best attitude to take?

Isn't it just possible that this change—your parent getting remarried—could be a healthy one? You can't be sure, of course, but won't you make things worse by storming into your room or by being rude to this new person?

Slamming the door and refusing to talk to either of them will not help you personally. It won't help your relationship with your parent. It will hurt your siblings. Even if you don't like it and you think this person is a real *nowhere* person, it is probably wiser to be gracious and cooperative.

If this new person is going to become a part of the family, you must not be the one who causes problems. Of course, if you have some very valid or strong doubts about this person, you should try to express these fears kindly and privately with your parent.

You'll be able to see if your feelings and remarks are appreciated or wanted. Hopefully, your parent will talk it over with you seriously.

Actually, it is considerate and nice for parents to discuss their future marriage plans with their children if they are old enough to understand and be reasonable. On the other hand, you can't expect a small child to make logical, adult decisions. Your parents must make the decisions.

Once again, the older children have to be careful. Sometimes parents may be trying to be fair by involving the children into the decision of whether or not to go ahead with marriage plans. This could be dangerous. If things don't go right, the children don't want to hear, "I married this person because you said you would be good."

Even if you are convinced that your parent should (or should not) go ahead and marry this person, you would do best to stay out of it. It's just another situation where you are not really qualified or able to help pick a stepparent. You are better off saying, "Gee, Mom, I know you are lonely, but I can't tell you what to do." Or, "Dad, I know you like to be with this person, but I can't tell you what is best."

If you remain calm and say it politely, you'll get through this period. You can, however, promise that if they decide to get married, you will try to be a good member of this changed (blended family). Hopefully, your parent will select a mate that will be an aid and comfort long after you have moved away.

You have to ask yourself something else. Ask yourself whether or not this new person that has come into your parent's life is likely to be there later on when you are gone. Is your parent better off having someone else?

Be careful. Don't decide that you don't like your mother's friend because he is too fat, too skinny, too bald, too short, too tall, or because the color of his hair is not what you like.

Don't hate your father's new love because she is too young, too old, too pretty, too ugly, or too tall. Don't be angry if she fusses over your dad too much. Don't decide that she has the wrong hair color. It could change in the morning.

Look at the person's values and attitudes. Is this person kind? Does this person work hard? Does he or she want what is best for the children? Is this person good to your parent?

Would things really be better if he or she were not in the picture?

Don't be too quick to judge. This new person might be especially kind and eager to share your interests. This new person might drop you off at the mall, take you shopping, or to your school games. Often the stepparent becomes a real help in taking you where you need to be.

Don't close the door to new people without just cause. Remember, too, that this will change for better or worse. Nothing stays the same. It is possible that your parent has chosen a fine person to join the family—cheerful, kind, and understanding.

In the meantime, it will be in the family's best interest and your best interest to give it a fair shot. To put obstacles in the way will only complicate things. If it doesn't work out—if the two adults don't get along with each other—it won't be your fault. You were kind and cooperative and were just trying to grow up sensibly. That's a mature attitude and a good way to deal with change.

Chapter 13
A Look Ahead

In a few minutes you will have finished reading this book, a book which should help you deal with your parents' divorce. Again, it is very important that you share these words with your parents—both of them.

If it is within your power to do, have them read this book from cover to cover. Suggest that they give up a television program or a movie to find time to read it. Offer to do the dishes or some other extra chore while they read this book. Your parents need to know a child's view of their divorce. They need to know what you are feeling as they go on with their divorce actions.

It will be so much easier for everyone concerned if your parents understand your fears and problems. They will make better decisions throughout their planning stages. In the meantime, hopefully you will have learned some basic ways to handle the disappointing situations that you may face.

> *It will be so much easier for everyone concerned if your parents understand your fears and problems.*

Your parents must come to understand that you should never be made to feel guilty when they go their separate ways. They should never ask you to chose one parent over the other unless you are truly old enough to make a wise choice. They should never put you in the middle of their quarrels.

Parents should realize that their children have a right to be with and to love the other parent. Parents should honor the visiting rights of the other parent and not make the visits difficult. They must take extra care in planning the holidays. They must not act as if you aren't supposed to love the other parent. Parents must not try to break the natural bond (love) that you have for both parents. You should be welcome at both homes without any arguments from the adults. Of course, if there has been sexual or physical abuse, this would change all the rules.

 Educational Media Corporation®

In any case, parents should not say terrible and mean things about each other. They must learn to control their emotions and their words. Words cannot be taken back. Parents should realize that it is the child that needs the comforting. The child should not have to do the parenting. At least parents should notice when the child is doing the parenting—taking on the adult's job. They could learn from the child.

At the same time, you must be as polite and understanding as possible. You will realize that being quarrelsome and rude does not help anyone. All of the parties involved must work at being reasonable.

You must also work hard at being the best child you know how to be. Don't neglect your studies. Don't be stubborn about doing chores around the house. Don't mope and sulk to get your way. Learn to discuss problems instead of avoid them.

It is true that your parents' divorce will bring about many, many changes, more than has been covered in this book. Remember the divorce does not have to change the important things, that of still being a family and still loving each other.

You will still be the child and they will still be your parents, even if they are living in different houses. You will love them and they will continue to love you. Your grandparents will still be your grandparents. Your brothers and sisters will still be your brothers and sisters.

You will see and visit both parents. Each will watch you grow and anxiously share the good things in your life as well as the problems. They will still be the grandparents of your children when you have children.

You will see that change is not always bad, but it is a necessary part of growing up. You may find that blending families (Brady Bunch children) can work out fairly well.

And, as you see yourself change, you may begin to understand your own feelings better. You will begin to develop a personal philosophy, a way of looking at life and handling various situations.

You will see what an important part you can play in dealing with the new people that come into your life. You will even begin to understand how others feel, especially your parents.

One or both of your parents may disappoint you. They may not do what good parents should do. As painful as it may become at times, you can handle it. You can look upon each problem and make plans for handling it.

If one parent abandons you, leaves you, or doesn't do the right thing, you will know it, but you will survive. The day will come when that parent will come to know your disappointment.

There will be time also for forgiveness—a chance to try again, if you wish. You will be older then. You will have made it through some tough times. You can pick up the pieces with the parent who abandoned you, or you can walk away. You'll be old enough to make the decision. The choice will be up to you.

Most of what happens to you during your parents' divorce will really be up to you. Your parents are taking a very big step, but you do not have to let it get you down. Their divorce does not have to change any of your goals. It may, in fact, cause you to grow up a bit faster and become a bit wiser.

Educational Media Corporation®

It may cause you to create some lifetime plans and develop some personal skills. You can learn from your parents' divorce and become a better parent yourself. You can become the kind of adult that you will respect and admire. You can still become what you want to become.

Smile, put aside your fears, and make a promise to yourself, right now, to make yours the best life possible.

Educational Media Corporation®